the Lexicon of Intent***** Ambiguous Recommendations

Positive-Sounding References for People Who Can't Manage Their Own Sock Drawers

Robert J. Thornton

Foreword by Richard Lederer

SOURCEBOOKS HYSTERIA™
AN IMPRINT OF SOURCEBOOKS, INC.®
NAPERVILLE, ILLINOIS

Published by Sourcebooks, Inc.
P.O. Box 4410, Naperville, Illinois 60567-4410
(630) 961-3900
FAX: (630) 961-2168
www.sourcebooks.com

Library of Congress Cataloging-in-Publication Data

Thornton, Robert J. (Robert James), 1943-
L.I.A.R. : the lexicon of intentionally ambiguous recommendations /
  Robert J. Thornton—2nd ed.
    p. cm.
Rev. ed of: Lexicon of intentionally ambiguous recommendations (LIAR).
  1998.
ISBN 1-4022-0139-7 (alk. paper)
1. Employment references—United States. 2. Employment references. I.
Title: Lexicon of intentionally ambiguous recommendations. II. Title:
LIAR. III. Thornton, Robert J. (Robert James), 1943- Lexicon of
intentionally ambiguous recommendations (LIAR). IV. Title.
HF5549.5.R45T46 2003
650.14'02'07—dc21

                                                    2003005241

Printed and bound in the United States of America
VP   10 9 8 7 6 5 4 3 2 1

To Julie, Jenni, and Bobby

CONTENTS

FOREWORD

by Richard Lederer, author of *Anguished English*

During a late and unlamented tax season, the H&R Block Company ran a commercial claiming that it "prepares more complex tax returns than any CPA firm in America."

Did this ad mean that the company prepares tax returns that are more complex (which is how most consumers interpreted the claim) or that it prepares a greater quantity of complex tax returns? Grammatically, does the adjective "more" modify "complex" or "returns"?

Challenged by the New York State Society of CPAs, an H&R Block assistant vice president said that the company defines "complex" as individual returns with schedules. He added that the qualification "makes it clear that H&R Block does not purport to prepare tax returns that are more complex than the tax returns prepared by CPA firms." Whether by accident or on purpose, H&R Block ended up with an ambiguous statement that just happened to serve their bottom line.

I believe that the H&R Block heads are disciples of *The Lexicon of Intentionally Ambiguous Recommendations,* a small classic by Robert J. Thornton. The corporation apparently learned from the examples in *L.I.A.R.* that language can fly in the face of the physical law that says two things can't occupy the same space at the same time. As you're about to see in abundance, two entirely opposite meanings can coexist in the same written territory.

It is that quirk of the English language on which Professor Thornton seizes, much to the benefit of those of us who are fated to provide testimony for those whom we teach, work with, are related to, or live near. Cobbling letters of recommendation is no easy task. Take it from me, who, during my twenty-eight years as an inmate in the house of correction of composition (a.k.a. an English teacher), was asked to write thousands of such statements.

But don't despair. A solution is at hand—and is apparently in your hands right now. Thornton's loopy guidebook uses cleverly push me–pull you words and phrases to steer a sane course between the Scylla of the desire to write an honest, informative recommendation and the Charybdis of the wrath of the recommendee and the threat of a lawsuit. This is how I learned to write worry-free about any disruptive dullard in my courses who possessed the temerity to want to attend a top college. I calmly bore witness that "he belongs in a class by himself."

I swear that I have not been paid to write this heartfelt foreword.

That's because the publisher knows that I am good for nothing.

I wanted to write this foreword very badly.

And now I have.

PREFACE

Back in 1987, I wrote an article that appeared in the *Chronicle of Higher Education* entitled "I Can't Recommend the Candidate Too Highly." The article contained a handful of humorous double-meaning phrases for letters of recommendation, and made reference to a (then mythical) *Lexicon of Inconspicuously Ambiguous Recommendations*. To my great surprise, the news media took a considerable interest in the "method" that I had devised for writing letters of recommendation that could be interpreted either positively or negatively. Theoretically, a writer of such a letter could convey honest information about the person being "recommended" without fear of a lawsuit—although my hope then and now is that no one would take my method *too* seriously.

Over the next several months, I wrote a book with the slightly altered title—*Lexicon of Intentionally Ambiguous Recommendations*—which was published by Meadowbrook in 1988. I continued to receive many calls and requests for the book long after it went out of print, and Almus Editions published a second edition in 1998. This revised second edition contains most of the material from the first, along with a large number of new entries in chapter 3 and a new chapter ("The Other Foot") showing how persons with lackluster credentials can make their credentials seem to…well, lack less luster.

The writing of each of the editions of the *Lexicon* has been great fun, and I have many people to thank for the ideas they passed on to me or the patience they showed (*most* of the time) in listening to my ideas. I've no doubt inadvertently left out a few names, but here goes: Rene Hollinger (who also typed and commented on the entire revised manuscript), Diane Oechsle, Jon Innes, Art King, Jim Hobbs, Revelly Paul, Tom and Jean Hyclak, Mike Kolchin, George Beezer, Bruce Smackey, Dick Barsness, Vince and Nancy Munley, Tony O'Brien, David Leahigh, Christy Roysdon, Wayne Coon, George Nation (double thanks), Pat Ward, Rich and Judy Aronson, Jim Hall, Jim Dearden, Larry Taylor, Frank Gunter, Todd Watkins, Jim Rebele, Judy McDonald, Colleen Callahan, Mary Deily, Roi Thomas, Malcolm Rees, David Greenaway, Charles Moyer, Harry Dower, Mike Hodges, Dan Ramsdell, Ray Larson, Larry Shankweiler, Fred Brubaker, Nicholas Balabkins, Steve Thode, and Pat D'Elia.

Special thanks should also go to Eli Schwartz, who spawned the first *L.I.A.R.* phrase; to Bill Johnson, whose timely press release generated widespread interest in the article in the *Chronicle*; to Peter How, Richard Chait, and Clark Kerr, for allowing me to use variants of their own ambiguous gems; to Bruce Lansky and Patricia McKernon, for their help and encouragement on the first edition; to Russell Robé, for launching the 1998 Almus edition; and to Peter Lynch and Dominique Raccah of Sourcebooks, for their enthusiasm and interest in seeing the *Lexicon* published once again. Richard Lederer (whose work I greatly admire) also deserves thanks for writing a foreword to this edition.

Finally, I'd like to express my gratitude to the members of my family who read through and commented on various versions of the manuscript (yawn!) or who offered encouragement: Julie, Jenni, Bobby, Brandt, Eliza, Kathy Fergus, Dorothy Menze, Mary Beth Balcarcel, Denise Watermann, Kathy Wadington, and Frank Roske. For their help, no amount of thanks will suffice.

—Robert J. Thornton

chapter one

THE LEGAL CONTEXT

The Big Sweat

You work for a major corporation, and you've just been asked to write a letter of recommendation for a coworker who wants a top management job at another firm. The problem is, you've worked with this person long enough to know that he can't manage his own sock drawer. What do you say? Do you tell him you don't think he's suitable for the position and that you can't give him a recommendation? (Remember, if he doesn't get the job, you have to continue working with him.) Or do you agree to write the recommendation and lie to the prospective employer about his qualifications?

You're a college professor, and, after a knock on your office door, in walks a student asking for a letter of recommendation for a job. Do you remember the student? Of course you do. She's the one who wrote on her examination paper in world history that Louis XIV was "King of the Sun," and chastised Martin Luther for nailing ninety-five theologians to a church door.[1] But the student has a pleasing personality—even if her view of history is somewhat warped—and also happens to be the dean's daughter. What do you do?

You're at home relaxing on your porch one evening, and your neighbor stops by to ask if you would agree to act as a character reference for him. Character reference? you think to yourself. This guy's a character, all right. He burned down his garage shooting off illegal fireworks, is loaded five nights a week, and played "Dueling Banjos" at his daughter's wedding. What do you say to him?

In any of these cases, you would probably write a favorable letter even when you know the candidate is mediocre or unqualified. Why? For several reasons. Many people (I among them) suffer from the "marshmallow syndrome," a chronic affliction that causes people to break out in a cold sweat, bite their nails, and lose sleep when they have to make a frank—but unfavorable—evaluation of another person. The problem has become far more widespread in recent years because more and more candidates are now exercising their legal right to read letters of recommendation. Many people are pursuing litigation if the contents are not to their liking and are poorly documented.

Litigation?

You bet. Consider the following cases:

- Mr. M. was fired. When he couldn't get work with other firms, he hired a detective to sniff out the recommendation

---

[1] See Anders Henriksson, "A History of the Past: 'Life Reeked with Joy,'" *Wilson Quarterly* (Spring, 1983), pp. 168–71.

given by his former employer. The detective found out that the former employer was referring to Mr. M. as "one of the dumbest employees he had ever had," adding that there was a "village out there that is missing an idiot." Mr. M. went on to sue his former employer for malicious defamation.

- Ms. R. had worked as a clerk-typist for a labor-relations company before quitting to move to a new area. While applying for another job, an interviewer confided to her that one of her letters of recommendation was very uncomplimentary. It seems that her former employer went on and on about her poor spelling, noting that her letters often referred to the "union representative" as the "onion representative." Ms. R. was incensed, took her employer to court, and wound up with about fifty thousand green ones—and we're not talking onions here.

- Mr. B. taught algebra for two years at a private high school and then decided to look elsewhere. When he had trouble getting an offer, he became suspicious and hired a service to check on what kind of reference letter he was getting from his former employer. The service reported that the principal described him as a "disaster in the classroom" with absolutely no control over his students. The letter went on to say that the blackboard in his classroom had attracted so many spitballs it looked like a stucco wall. Mr. B. exercised his right to sue and "stuccoed" his former employer for $100,000 with punitive damages for malice.

In a nutshell, letters of recommendation are no longer confidential. What's more, people on the receiving end of unfavorable letters of recommendation are increasingly apt to sue—successfully, too. What's happening as a result? More and more firms are unwilling to provide prospective employers of former workers with any more information than "name, rank, and serial number." In other words, they simply verify the fact that the person once worked there, in this or that capacity, for so long a period of time. Increasingly, employment consultants are advising firms to clam up on recommendations.

Maybe this is all right, you might say. Perhaps letters of recommendation should be abolished as a requirement of employment, but I don't think so. The fact remains that firms simply have no *potentially* better means of gaining reliable information about a candidate's qualifications than through people who have had close contact with him or her. Even firms that refuse to provide letters of recommendation for their own former employees apparently believe this. At the same time that they refuse to give information about former employees, they often continue to require and check references of those whom they do employ.[2]

It's in their best interest to do so because they're being squeezed by litigation from current employees as well. In one recent case, an employee who was assaulted by a fellow employee sued the firm for not researching the other employee's record more thoroughly before hiring him. In another case involving violent behavior, the victim sued both the current employer *and* the former employer of the alleged assailant (or "perp" as in police talk). The reason

---

[2] "Reference Checking: What's the Point When Everyone Is Afraid to Talk?" *Wall Street Journal*, 5 May 1987, p. 1.

offered was that the former employer had knowledge of the person's violent tendencies and thus could have avoided the catastrophe by disclosing such information.

Because of cases like these, employers now find themselves between a rock and a hard place. Giving bad references often leads to lawsuits—so employers don't want to give references. But not seeking out references or not providing truthful ones can also lead to lawsuits if some employees harm other employees or the public. What to do?

The Lexicon

Obviously, employers should be able to write recommendations without fear of lawsuits. They need a way to convey honest—though perhaps unfavorable—information about a candidate for a job *without the candidate being able to prove or even perceive it as such.* To this end, I have designed the *Lexicon of Intentionally Ambiguous Recommendations—L.I.A.R.*, for short. Two samples from the lexicon should illustrate the approach:

- *To describe a candidate who is not very industrious:* "In my opinion, you will be very fortunate to get this person to work for you."
- *To describe a candidate who is certain to foul up any project:* "I am sure that whatever task he undertakes—no matter how small—he will be fired with enthusiasm."

Phrases like these allow an evaluator to offer a negative opinion of the candidate's personal qualities, work habits, or motivation, yet enable the candidate to believe that he or she has been praised highly.

The phrases in the lexicon are not simply vague or ambiguous. Rather, they convey a double meaning that can be interpreted as either high praise or damning criticism. In this way, they satisfy everyone. The writer can sleep without feeling guilty about having compromised his or her principles ("I told it like it was...well, almost.") *and* without fear of being slapped with a lawsuit. The person for whom the recommendation was written is at best pleased ("Gee, Harry wrote me a very nice letter.") or at worst perplexed ("Just what *did* he mean by saying I will be 'fired with enthusiasm'?"). And the recipient of the letter? How is he or she to interpret the ambiguous recommendation? Any way at all!

chapter two

THE L.I.A.R. GUIDE

Getting Started

Maybe now you're convinced of the potential value of ambiguous letters of recommendation. But are they easy to write? Well, with a little assistance and a bit of practice, you'll find that they are.

In this chapter you will learn some tricks to the art—or more appropriately the *craft*—of writing ambiguously. For, although the lexicon in the next chapter is large, many more undiscovered ambiguous references probably exist out there in the vast verbal universe. And with a bit of practice dangling participles, mutilating punctuation marks, and executing typographical errors, soon you'll be crafting your own ambiguous recommendations.

You'll learn several ways to write ambiguously. For example, you can mess up the syntax, or structure, of a sentence. You can punctuate it obscurely. Or you can intentionally make confusing typos. I'll walk you through each device and explain carefully how to create maximum confusion.

Syntactical Ambiguity

If you remember your high-school English class, you will recall Miss Grundy warning you of the dangers of misplaced modifiers—particularly dangling participles. (As a young boy, I thought that dangling a participle was a mortal sin.) Dangling participles are modifiers that seem to refer to two different words or to a word that isn't even in the sentence. As such, they can be used to create double meanings. Consider this one:

> "The volume of work that Mr. Smith performs, while staggering, is only a fraction of what he is capable of doing."

The participle "staggering," in this sentence, is dangling. The reader is not sure just who or what is staggering here— Mr. Smith (who may enjoy an occasional nip on the job) or the workload that he handles.

Here's another example:

> "He had a lot of brass pushing for his promotion."

This misplaced modifier "pushing"—again a participle— could either be construed as modifying "brass" (meaning that his promotion had the support of the bigwigs upstairs) or "he" (which would turn a flattering statement into a negative one).

Misplacing modifiers is not so hard to do, but getting your participles to dangle ambiguously is difficult. Miss Grundy was a tough cookie, and reversing learned behavior is not easy. You may be comforted to know that the ability to dangle participles is not genetically inherited. It simply requires practice. Therefore, the person who aspires to create ambiguous phrases is encouraged to engage in regular dangling exercises—five per day to start, working up to twenty per day. Sometimes it helps to dangle them with a friend.

Ambiguous Punctuation

The Quomma

A wide variety of ambiguous recommendations can be written using a little known (as yet) punctuation mark called a "questionable comma"—or "quomma" for short. It looks like a comma but also could be mistaken for, say, a small coffee stain, a defect in the paper, or maybe even a dead gnat or fruit fly.

The quomma takes many forms, but often looks like this:

ı

or like this: **ʼ**
or like this: **➔**

You get the idea. The reader thinks it might be a comma, but can't be sure if it really is a comma or something else entirely.

In what types of situations is the quomma valuable? It's especially handy whenever a phrase or sentence would have one meaning if the mark were really a comma and another meaning if not.

This is all very theoretical, so let's use a few examples. Suppose the writer of a recommendation wishes to make an ambiguous statement about a lazy person in whom he or she has little confidence. The writer could state in a letter:

> "He won't do anything which will lower your high regard for him."

Read without internal punctuation, the sentence seems to convey high praise and indicates that the candidate's performance will very likely live up to his prospective employer's expectations. However, if a comma is inserted between the words "anything" and "which," the sentence becomes:

> "He won't do anything, which will lower your high regard for him."

The commas have changed a sentence of high praise to one of damning criticism.[1]

Herein lies the utility of the quomma: it renders the sentence ambiguous. If a quomma is inserted between two critical words, the reader of the recommendation cannot tell whether it is truly a comma or not, and can interpret the sentence positively or negatively.

You might wonder why I've been so vague about the exact appearance or shape of the quomma. The reason is this: to be useful, the quomma must cause confusion as to whether it is

---

[1] Some grammar hawks would argue that "which" should be used only to introduce nonrestrictive clauses and "that" should be used to introduce restrictive clauses. However, several usage guides suggest that "which" is acceptable with either type of clause. (For example, see Hodges' *Harbrace College Handbook* and *Fowler's Modern English Usage*.)

or is not a comma. This is particularly true when quommas must be used in tandem, as in the following sentence:

"Her record speaks well of her." [High praise]

or

"Her record speaks, well, of her." [A "nothing" comment]

Clearly, using two quommas so close together would cause suspicion if they assumed the same shape. Therefore, for those recommendations that use the quomma, I will simply use the letter Q to indicate appropriate quomma placement, as in the following sentence:

"His credentials are nothingQ which should be laughed at."

Not only does the Q help the reader to recognize where this all-important punctuation mark must be placed, but it also makes the typesetter's work easier, since he has no quomma symbols and the press has a shortage of gnats and fruit flies.[2]

The Schizocolon

With a little imagination, you can use a semicolon to generate the same type of confusion as the quomma. For example, take the next sentence:

---

[2] Helpful hint: allowing a banana to age gracefully in your briefcase over a period of several months is one surefire way to allow the fruitfly population to (excuse me) be fruitful and multiply.

"Once he put his mind to a problem, he wouldn't stop until he had solved it."

Sounds like high praise? Just the type of employee you'd love to have working for you? Of course. But what if the comma after "problem" was a semicolon instead? Then the sentence would imply that most of the time the guy's mind was in low gear, but that one time—just one time—he really did apply himself. In fact, this "schizophrenic semicolon" (or "schizocolon" for short) can be used effectively in a large number of sentences and phrases involving the word "once." For example:

"Once he came to work; he was all business."
"Once he actually made a decision; he took great satisfaction from it."
"Once she gave up smoking; she was a much more productive employee."

Writers who take delight in the schizocolon form it in various ways. Some actually type in the semicolon (and later blame secretaries for the mistake). Others partially erase the upper half (the period) of the semicolon, leaving the reader to wonder which punctuation mark it really is. Still others apply a very small dollop of walnut-fudge topping for the upper half of the semicolon to cause maximum bewilderment. In the lexicon that follows, schizocolons will be noted with the symbol **᠈**.

Quommas and schizocolons are not the only types of ambiguous punctuation marks in the lexicon. Sprinkled throughout, for example, you'll find "is-it-or-isn't-it hyphens." (I chose not to invent another cutesy term like "quomma" for the is-it-or-isn't-it hyphen for fear we'd all start sounding like Elmer Fudd.) The creative user can fashion other types of ambiguous punctuation marks as the need arises.

The Space Oddity

A great many ambiguous phrases can result from ambiguous spacing. For instance, a letter of recommendation might read:

> "Whenever there is a tough task at hand, this person is usually outstanding."

To render this phrase ambiguous, the typist should insert a half-space (or what I call a "space oddity") between the first t and the s in "outstanding." That way, the reader will be unsure whether the person handles pressure well, or—if the space is taken literally—perhaps whenever important work needs to be done the person is usually out standing somewhere else, maybe having a cigarette.

Let's try one more. How about this one?

> "In what ways did he distinguish himself? In competent dealings with customers and in considerate behavior toward his coworkers."

In the lexicon (chapter 3), words requiring the use of a space oddity will be written with a slash (/).

The Negative Overload

Have you ever seen a sentence like the one following?

> "I sincerely doubt that there is anyone who would fail to deny his not inconsiderable contributions to our firm."

"Huh?" you're probably saying to yourself. "I'd better read it again." There are so many negative or near-negative words in the sentence that it is completely unclear whether the writer is complimenting or trashing the guy's record. Or how about this one?

> "It is not very difficult to argue against the contention that without him we would hardly have been in the situation we are in today."

So how do you unravel the meanings of the two sentences above—or write one of your own? There is one way that will *usually* work. Remember that the negative of a negative statement is a positive statement. And the negative of a negative of a negative statement (whew!) is still a negative statement. In other words, if there are an *even* number of negative terms, the negatives cancel out, and the statement becomes a positive one. An odd number of negatives? The statement is negative. I hope you're still with me and haven't yet thrown down this book in disgust. I said above that this will *usually* work, but words like "doubt" and "hardly" make the interpretation more confusing still. So just what *are* the two recommendations above—good or bad? I honestly don't know. I've read them three times and *still* can't figure them out.

One final word of caution: some people with poor grammatical training often use pairs of negatives in sentences like the following:

"He didn't do nothin' right."

or

"I ain't heard nothing good about him."

Both are, of course, grammatically incorrect and imply negative statements despite the presence of an even number of negatives. But if you do express yourself like this, you really shouldn't be writing letters of recommendation at all. Instead, you should be shot—or, even worse, be forced to repeat the first grade (with no recess).

Now Then...

After this little venture into grammatical deep space, you are ready to tackle the lexicon. Who knows? With a little practice you might one day receive the coveted Weasel Award—the *L.I.A.R.* enthusiast's equivalent of the black belt. In any case, becoming a master of the ambiguous letter of recommendation is virtually guaranteed to bring with it one further benefit: once your prowess is known, rarely will you be asked to write letters of recommendation. Come to think of it, I haven't been asked to write a single one since I wrote this book!

chapter three

THE LEXICON

This chapter contains about 350 ambiguous sentences and phrases you can use in letters of recommendation. Most of them convey opposite meanings—high praise or damning criticism. Some, however, are simply wishy-washy, or what I call "nothing" recommendations. Their alternate meaning is not really bad, but rather…well, not much of anything.

The lexicon covers fifteen categories of common employee problems:

- Absenteeism
- Alcohol/Drug Problems
- Character Defects
- Criminal Background
- Disagreeableness
- Dishonesty
- Incompetence
- Lack of Ambition
- Laziness

- Loose Morals
- Mediocrity
- Misfit
- Stupidity
- Unemployability
- Unreliability
- Miscellany

A final section contains recommendations for people with less-common problems, such as size 16E feet. (I can hear you snickering, but who knows when the need might arise for such a recommendation?)

Where appropriate, items will be footnoted to point out quommas, space oddities, schizocolons, or other devices for creating ambiguity. The footnotes will be especially useful for those lazy readers who did not do their homework and skipped over the L.I.A.R. Guide (chapter 2) before tackling the lexicon.

ABSENTEEISM

Recommendation	*Meaning*
"A man like him is hard to find."	We have no idea where he hides.
"She's not your every/day employee." [1]	…every *other* day, maybe.
"Once he came to work ⸹ he was all business." [2]	We never saw him again after that.
"When I knew her, it seemed that her career was just taking off."	…taking off for the shore, for the ball game, for the rest of the week….
"He was the most conscientious, if not the most punctualQ person I've ever worked with." [3]	Well, was he punctual or not?
"Your worries will be over when he starts working for you."	Our worries certainly were over when he would start. He often didn't arrive until noon.
"She was always there when we needed her."	We wish she would have been *here*, though.

---

[1] For an explanation of the space oddity, see p. 13.
[2] For a discussion of the schizocolon (⸹), see p. 11.
[3] For an explanation of the quomma (Q) and its uses, see p. 9.

ALCOHOL/DRUG PROBLEMS

Recommendation	Meaning
"The volume of work he performs, while staggering, is still only a fraction of what he can do."	Imagine how much he could do if he were sober.
"I would say that his real talent is getting wasted at his current job."	He gets bombed regularly.
"He often went through several drafts before he thought his reports sounded just right."	He works better with a couple of beers under his belt.
"She was always high in my opinion."	I don't know what she was on.
"He works with as much speed as he can."	He's always popping pills.
"We remember the hours he spent working with us as happy hours."	He was usually sloshed.
"She's a seasoned employee."	She's usually pickled, in fact.
"We generally found him loaded with work to do."	He'd usually get tanked before he'd work.
"He is a man of great visions."	He hallucinates.

"He is never tight with his money."

He prefers to get loaded on other people's money.

"He once had an alcohol problem, but I understand that he doesn't drink any more."

He doesn't drink any less either.

"I'd make sure there are no bars in the way of this man coming to work for you."

He's likely to stop in for a few belts before showing up at the office.

CHARACTER DEFECTS

Recommendation	*Meaning*
"He worked for us for twenty odd years."	He's a very strange person.
"There is always a method to his madness."	He isn't *just* insane.
"I'd say that she was awed/odd by our firm's standards." [4]	A very strange person.
"All of us had a rather good impression of him."	...but there was this one guy who could mimic him perfectly.
"No matter what type of work you give her, I have no doubt that you will soon find her committed."	She's a certified lunatic and belongs in an institution.
"You'll be very impressed with his performance at work."	He's really quite a convincing actor.
"She gives every appearance of being a reliable, conscientious employee."	...but appearances are deceiving.

[4] This sentence uses a homophone and works only for oral recommendations. For a discussion of homophones, see p. 95.

"He doesn't mind being disturbed."

He sees his therapist far less often than he should.

"He usually works in a frenzy."

The guy is a maniac.

"I think you can say that he gave our office its character."

And what a character he was!

"This man should go very far."

Help him out. Pack his bags.

"I can't begin to tell you what a fine person he is."

I can't even *think* about beginning to tell you.

"He's an expert at considering multiple opinions."

In other words, he's indecisive.

"I would call her a top psychologist."

But please call one... immediately.

CRIMINAL BACKGROUND

Recommendation	Meaning
"He's a man of many convictions."	In fact, he's got a criminal record a mile long.
"He had a somewhat troubled past, but I'd say that now he's turned his life around 360 degrees."	In other words, he's right back where he started.
"While he worked with us he was given numerous citations."	He was arrested many times.
"I'm sorry we let her get away."	We should have prosecuted.
"She has a long and notable record."	The police know her well.
"He honestly felt that his previous position was too confining."	He did time in the Big House.
"It won't take long for him to break in at your place."	He's burglarized every other place he's worked at.
"He's the type of man I'd want to have in a hard sell/cell situation." [5]	...and throw away the key.

---

[5] This sentence uses a homophone and works only for oral recommendations. For a discussion of homophones, see p. 95.

"When he worked for us he would transport iron and steel/steal from our warehouse." [6]

He robbed us blind.

---

[6] Ibid.

DISAGREEABLENESS

Recommendation	*Meaning*
"It's been a good two years since he left our employ."	His leaving was the best thing that ever happened to us.
"It absolutely amazes me how he can work with others."	...because personally I find him disgusting.
"I am pleased to say that he is a former colleague of mine."	I can't tell you how happy I am that he left our firm.
"The breadth/breath of the man is overwhelming and quite obvious to those who work closely with him." [7]	He's got the worst halitosis you'll ever experience.
"He's always trying."	He'll get on your nerves.
"You won't find many people like her."	In fact, most people detest her.
"One usually comes away from him with a good feeling."	He's a most unpleasant person.
"You'll find him a difficult man to replace."	He'll sue if you try to fire him.

---

[7] This sentence uses a homophone and works only for oral recommendations. For a discussion of homophones, see p. 95.

"You can ask him to do anything and he won't mind."

He won't do what you ask, but he won't mind your asking.

"She's one of the most discriminating people you'll ever meet."

She hates African-Americans, Hispanics, Asians…almost everybody.

"There's no questioning his abilities."

He gets angry if you do.

"He will take full advantage of his staff."

He even has one of them mowing his lawn on weekends.

"I could never give her enough credit for the job she did for us."

She always wanted more.

"He had a lot of brass pushing for his promotion."

He's got a lot of nerve.

"It was a crying shame when she left our firm."

What an ugly scene she made.

"It was a pleasure working with her for the short time that I did."

Thank God it wasn't longer.

"He takes a lot of enjoyment out of work."

…and ruins it for others, too.

"Her input was always critical."

She never had a good word to say.

"When this young man left our employ, we were quite hopeful he would go a long way with his skills."

We prayed that he'd go as far away as possible.

"There's not a person in the office who could fault her work."

She would sulk if they did.

"Most everyone here used to call her Mother."

Until her Mother got an unlisted phone number.

"I would put this student in a class by himself."

His aroma was that offensive.

"It's sad to see so many workers like her leaving."

But they were ecstatic when she finally went.

"In/sensitivity and in/consideration toward others—in these characteristics he was remarkable" [8]

He didn't give a damn about anyone.

"He enjoys a good wine/whine from time to time." [9]

What a complainer!

---

[8] For an explanation of the space oddity (/), see p. 13.
[9] This sentence uses a homophone and works only for oral recommendations. For a discussion of homophones, see p. 95.

"There was much to·do in her division when we hired her as manager." [10]	Everyone was upset.
"I can't say anything bad about him."	I'm afraid to.
"She doesn't mind authority."	She just does what she wants.
"He works furiously whenever he faces an important deadline."	He gets very angry when he is rushed.
"He is a self-made man." [11]	...mainly because nobody else would help him.
"We were amazed when she resigned. We didn't think she would ever leave the firm."	It was about time, though.
"He's the type of worker who just won't quit."	...so we had to fire him.
"From the first day she began working with us, no one has shown any more interest in our business."	She's driven away all our customers.

---

[10] The ambiguous punctuation mark used between to and do is called an "is-it-or-isn't-it hyphen." See p. 12

[11] Oscar Levant used this line.

"Most of his staff would like to see a picture of him hanging in the president's office some day."

Actually, they wouldn't care if he were shot, drowned, or pushed out a window.

"She stressed a smoothly functioning office."

Most of her staff was so stressed that they needed counseling.

"She has great skills in dealing with other people, and she is not at all reluctant to use them."

She used me and she'll use you.

"We all miss not seeing him at work."

This does *not* mean that we miss seeing him. We miss *not* seeing him.

"As far as his ability to work well with others, let me say that he stands alone in this regard."

Who would want to work with him?

"There was not a single note of discord when he worked for us."

It was a chorus.

"It is hard to imagine that anyone could fail to be impressed by or like Mr. Smedley."

He'll make quite an impression, but certainly no one will like him.

"He has the ability to turn on his staff."

He certainly turned on me. He never speaks to me anymore.

"No one comes close to him."

He's that offensive.

DISHONESTY

Recommendation	Meaning
"His résumé is too good to be true."	Actually, most of it *isn't* true.
"He won't give you lame excuses for his shortcomings."	They'll be whoppers.
"He's the type of man who takes everything with good humor."	He'll gladly steal the pants off you.
"Even though her work record was only average, her true ability was deceiving."	She was quite adept at lying.
"He left us with nearly one million dollars last year."	He ran off under suspicion of larceny.
"I'm not sure why he left, but there were rumors that he just couldn't take any more."	He took just about everything that wasn't nailed down.
"You simply won't believe this woman's credentials."	She faked most of her résumé.
"Give him the opportunity and he will forge a name for himself."	Don't leave any blank checks lying around.

"He gave a plausible explanation for the discrepancy in his books, which was later found to be made up."

He fabricated the whole story.

"As honest as the day is long."

This phrase is best used in letters written in December, preferably on the twenty-first.

"The man is simply an unbelievable worker."

You can't trust him for a minute.

"I never knew herQ to be dishonest." [12]

To be honest, I knew her.

"He always said that a little honesty goes a long way."

A *very* little honesty.

"It just didn't happen that he rose to the rank of vice president in only three years."

Like I said, it just didn't happen.

"He had a hand in our company's financial dealings."

Sticky fingers, actually.

---

[12] For an explanation of the quomma (Q) and its uses, see p. 9.

"I know himQ to be honest, and I know himQ to be frank." [13]

Yep, I know him. (This "nothing" recommendation also works well for guys named...you guessed it.)

"She merits a close look."

Don't let her out of your sight.

"He's just plain/playin' honest." [14]

Oh yes, he's the Great Pretender.

"At least two other major companies are after him."

The finance company and the electric company.

---

[13] Ibid.

[14] This phrase uses a homophone and works only for oral recommendations. For a discussion of homophones, see p. 95.

INCOMPETENCE

Recommendation	Meaning
"I recommend this man with no qualifications whatsoever."	He's woefully inept.
"I understand that she would very much like to work with you if possible."	She just can't seem to get herself moving, though.
"No amount of praise would suffice for the job that he's done for us."	He's bungled everything he ever tried to do.
"Her former boss was always raving about her work."	Her mistakes nearly drove him insane.
"He would always ask if there was anything he could do."	And we would always ask ourselves the same question.
"His value to the firm is, if anything, far greater than others who have held his position."	He may not be worth much, but the others before him were even worse.
"He has completed his schooling, and is now ready to strike out in a career."	I expect his batting average to be .000.
"I wouldn't hesitate to give her an unqualified recommendation."	She just doesn't have the skills for the job.

"We hope to find a suitable match for the job he performed for us."	Hold the match. Maybe a shredder would be better.
"When he was here, there wasn't much workQ which he couldn't do." [15]	He couldn't even succeed at small tasks.
"There was an overwhelming amount of responsibilityQ for her." [16]	Anyone *else* could have managed it easily.
"His credentials are nothingQ which should be laughed at." [17]	The guy's qualifications are a joke.
"You will soon find yourself happy to have her on board."	...a one-way bus to Peoria.
"You'll never see this man spoiled by success."	...because it's unlikely he'll ever be successful.
"This job requires few skillsQ which he lacks." [18]	There's almost nothing he can do.

---

[15] For an explanation of the quomma (Q) and its uses, see p. 9.
[16] Ibid.
[17] Ibid.
[18] Ibid.

"We were teetering on the threshold of bankruptcy last year, but his efforts pulled us through."

...to a state of bankruptcy, that is.

"She is resigning a position that she has held with our firm for many years; I truly wish there were more people like her."

...who would also resign.

"I would emphasize his performance in the following areas: in/capable managerial skills, in/decisive actions, and in/correct judgments." [19]

He can't seem to do *anything* right.

"We see a brilliant career ahead of her."

...far ahead of her.

"For the services he has rendered to our firm over the years, we find ourselves deeply indebted."

In fact, because of him we're now in hock up to our ears.

---

[19] For an explanation of the space oddity (/), see p. 13.

"There are no·accounts that I would hesitate to put this man in charge of." [20]

He could mess up *anybody*.

"She works without direction."

She's the most disorganized person you'll ever find.

"There was no limit to the credit she was given while working for us."

And now she's got every bill-collection agency in town after her.

"His list of achievements was...uh...laudable/lotta bull." [21]

He lied about most everything on his résumé.

"I can't remember ever hearing a single colleague complain about her work."

They generally sent a delegation.

"The attention he devotes to details is not excessive."

...to say the least.

"We are looking for great things from him."

...but we can't find them.

---

[20] The ambiguous punctuation mark used between no and accounts is called an "is-it-or-isn't-it hyphen." See p. 12.

[21] This phrase uses a homophone and works only for oral recommendations. For a discussion of homophones, see p. 95.

"From her very first day I had discussed/disgust with her plans for improving our sales." [22]

Her recommendations were simply ridiculous.

"He successfully raised/razed our standards of excellence." [23]

He made a shambles out of them.

"He had nothing to prove to us."

And he proved it.

"I will put down his accomplishments in a letter."

As I'll explain in the letter, they amounted to nothing.

"We wish we had ten employees like him."

Unfortunately, we have twenty.

"I'm sure he will show you the same disdain for laziness and incompetence that he showed us."

He has no tolerance for laziness, but his incompetence will soon be evident.

"He was instrumental in ru_ning our entire operation." [24]

Running...or ruining?

---

[22] Ibid.
[23] Ibid.
[24] The case of the missing letter.

"I'd say that his accomplishments were unheard of."

And unseen also.

"He wanted to work for us in the worst way."

And he did.

"After ten years on the job I'd say that he has certainly demonstrated his competence."

It's just too bad that it took him ten years to do so.

"All good managers want to eliminate problems, and he is certainly one of them."

One of the problems, that is.

"He filled a much-needed void in our work force."

We wish we still had that void.

"His digital capabilities are notable."

In other words, he's all thumbs.

LACK OF AMBITION

Recommendation	Meaning
"Whenever I would ask her to do something quickly, it usually took a second to complete it."	...a second person, that is.
"Once she got started on a project ⸙ she wouldn't stop until it was finished." [25]	It's the only thing she actually did in all the years she was with us.
"He couldn't care less about the number of hours he had to put in."	We just wish he could have cared more about them.
"He is not the type to run away from responsibility."	He'll walk very quickly, though.
"From the moment he arrives at work, he is ready to go."	...home.
"Whenever there is a tough task at hand, she is usually out/standing." [26]	...out standing somewhere else.
"She didn't think much of the extra time she had to work."	In fact, she didn't do much thinking during her regular work hours.

---

[25] For an explanation of the schizocolon (⸙), see p. 11.

[26] For an explanation of the space oddity (/), see p. 13.

"Is he enthusiastic about working? He wants to work just so much."

...and then take a nap or maybe leave early.

"The old adage, 'A woman's work is never done,' certainly sizes up what she did for us."

She never finished a thing.

"His principal ambition was to get a/head in his department." [27]

He hated to have to use the washroom down the hall.

"She commands the respect of everyone with whom she works."

...but she rarely gets it.

"Success won't go to his head."

How could it? He's never had any.

"She just might be the best accountant your firm has ever hired."

Then again, she might not.

"He only began working for us last year."

But he's been here since 1990.

"He doesn't do something just because he has to."

He doesn't do it because he doesn't *want* to.

---

[27] For an explanation of the space oddity (/), see p. 13.

"Would he be willing to work long hours? Let me just say that you won't find him wanting."

...to work long hours.

"He doesn't miss work."

Furthest thing from his mind.

"This guy's a real sleeper."

z-z-z-z

"I remember well the time he worked for us."

It was June 3, 2003, 10:15 A.M.

"He can usually bore right to the heart of the matter."

You'll never meet a duller person.

"He won't do anythingＱ which will cause your firm to lose money." [28]

His performance level is nil.

"It is hard to overstate his contributions."

It would also be hard to understate them.

"We expect much more from her in the future."

Heaven knows we didn't get much from her in the past.

"Most just show up for a paycheck, but few really earn it. He's certainly one of them."

...one of the former.

---

[28] For an explanation of the quomma (Ｑ) and its uses, see p. 9.

LAZINESS

Recommendation	Meaning
"You will be very fortunate to get this person to work for you."	She's not very industrious.
"He could not have done a better job for us if he had tried."	He's not only incompetent, but he's lazy as well.
"I think it's safe to say that his true interests were lying in the stockroom."	He used to sneak naps there.
"No job is too much for this man to handle."	He just can't seem to deal with any kind of responsibility.
"She works effortlessly."	She doesn't expend much energy.
"You will never catch him asleep on the job."	He's too crafty to get caught.
"He always found his work challenging."	He had such trouble understanding even the simplest things.
"She doesn't think twice about attacking a difficult problem."	In fact, she doesn't think about it at all.

"He spared no effort in his work." | He did as little as possible.

"You should seriously consider initiating an offer, since he probably won't apply himself." | He certainly didn't apply himself to anything *we* ever asked him to do.

"She always worked without a care." | If she made a mistake, so what!

"About his motivation? He is literally driven to work." | His wife drives him to the office.

"He would like nothing better than working for you." | He would rather do nothing at all.

"The volume of work that he performed was, if anything, much more than we expected." | Did he ever do anything? I really don't know.

"How would I describe him as a worker? Definitely over/ achieving."[29] | His achieving days are long gone.

"You'll be lucky to find her type." | She wouldn't type when she worked for us.

---

[29] For an explanation of the space oddity (/), see p. 13.

"In his work there was nothing to complain about."

...because he did literally nothing.

"She never seems to have too much work to do."

...so she plays a lot of computer games.

"He won't waste any time at work."

He probably won't even show up.

"He will never do anythingϘ which will disappoint you." [30]

The guy's a lazy bum, as you'll find to your dismay.

"She has sometimes been cited/sighted at her job." [31]

Once in a while she decides to come to work.

"He was never too far from the center of intellectual activity."

The farther the better.

"I would pursue the possibility of her working for you."

There's just a *chance* she might do something.

"Once he put his mind to his work§ nothing could stop him." [32]

Except for that one time, he was virtually worthless.

---

[30] For an explanation of the quomma (Ϙ) and its uses, see p. 9.

[31] This phrase uses a homophone and works only for oral recommendations. For a discussion of homophones, see p. 95.

[32] For a discussion of the schizocolon (§), see p. 10.

"He was with our firm a few years back, but I can't remember the exact dates he worked for us." | I think he might have shown up once or twice.

"He thinks little of hard work." | We wish he'd think more of it.

"He will do nothingQ which will lower your high regard for him." [33] | He's definitely a loafer.

"She's not averse to working over/time." [34] | She won't mind doing it...eventually.

"I'm sure this man would leap at the chance to work for you." | ...leap out the door, that is.

"She's workingQ for a changeQ in her position." [35] | It's about time she did something.

"He works best under pressure." | ...under the pressure of getting canned.

"The impression he conveys to others is no act." | He really *doesn't* do very much.

---

33. For an explanation of the quomma (Q) and its uses, see p. 9.
34. For an explanation of the space oddity (/), see p. 13.
35. Ibid.

"When he worked for us he never did anything halfway."

...although we'd have taken even that.

"He's not the type of person to simply go through the motions of looking busy at work."

He won't even do that.

"He always finds a way out of the most difficult problems."

He avoids them.

"She worked for us more or less for a year."

Actually, it was hard to tell just what she was doing for us.

"Most people he works with would like to have/halve his salary." [36]

He's paid twice as much as he's worth.

"You haven't seen anything yet."

And you probably won't, either.

---

[36] This phrase uses a homophone and works only for oral recommendations. For a discussion of homophones, see p. 95.

LOOSE MORALS[37]

Recommendation	Meaning
"It was a pleasure working under him."	X
"He will give you everything he's got on the job."	X
"I remember him as very often laidQ back when I first began working with him." [38]	X
"He scores well in an academic setting."	X
"He's broad-minded."	X
"I am confident she will make out on her new job."	X
"She's the kind of employee you can swear by."	X
"She was sad to leave all those workers who dearly loved her behind."	X

---

[37] Do not read this section if you are under sixteen (unless you are accompanied by an adult). The recommendations here do not require the usual set of translations.

[38] For an explanation of the quomma (Q) and its uses, see p. 9.

"He had good relations with his entire staff."	X
"Her trademark was in/decent dealings with others." [39]	X
"He touched most of those with whom he worked."	X
"He's a hands-on type."	X
"She's willing to bear/bare anything for the sake of her career." [40]	X
"He believes in a horizontal style of management."	X

---

[39] For an explanation of the space oddity (/), see p. 13.

[40] This phrase uses a homophone and works only for oral recommendations. For a discussion of homophones, see p. 95.

MEDIOCRITY

Recommendation	Meaning
"Waste no time in making this candidate an offer of employment."	She's not worth further consideration.
"All in all, I cannot recommend this person too highly."	He has lackluster credentials.
"You can't offer this man too high a salary."	You're better off saving your money.
"I can't give him enough credit for the job he's done for us over the years."	...certainly not enough for you to consider hiring him.
"We were forever asking him for new ideas."	We were sick and tired of the old ones.
"I would like to say that I am extremely impressed with her abilities."	...but I can't.
"She has made immeasurable contributions to our firm."	Far too minor to be measured.
"He deserves just recognition as a member of our work force."	...not praise, not a promotion, but just recognition.

"In all the discussions we had over the years, his salary never came up."

We never gave him a raise.

"She has a flair for writing."

She owns a felt-tipped pen.

"His record speaksQ wellQ of him." [41]

Whom else would it speak of?

"He's a man of vision."

He can see.

"Whenever he asked us for a raise, we usually let him have it."

We tossed him right out of the office.

"She workedQ wellQ with others." [42]

Everyone at our firm worked with other employees.

"Whatever he did for us, we were pleased with him."

I still don't know just what he did, though.

"When this man walks through the office door in the morning, he comes to work."

Where else would the door lead?

"All in all, I might strongly suggest that she be thought eligible for consideration."

Talk about a "nothing" recommendation!

---

[41] For an explanation of the quomma (Q) and its uses, see p. 9.
[42] Ibid.

"He has an eye for details." | In fact, he has two of them.

"How did he manage those who worked under him? Quite fairly." | ...Not well, not badly, just fairly.

"She has a real head on her shoulders." | At least she did the last time I looked.

"The money you will invest in training her will beQ wellQ spent." [43] | Well, uh, okay.

"He is always behind his fellow employees." | Slowest worker we've ever had.

"We usually passed on all her suggestions." | You'll pass on them too.

"Given his recent work, I would expect that his reputation in the future could only improve." | There's no other direction it could go.

"I sincerely doubt that there is anyone who would fail to deny his not inconsiderable contributions to our firm." | Huh?

---

[43] For an explanation of the quomma (Q) and its uses, see p. 9.

"If you're saying she has great potential, I couldn't agree with you more."

In fact, I couldn't agree with you at all.

"His performance didn't vary much. Each year usually looked like the last one."

Each year *should* have been the last one for him.

"I would place him among the top 95 percent of students that I've taught over the years."

Statistically speaking, he's a loser.

MISFIT

Recommendation	Meaning
"Once you hire him you'll see how important it is to have more qualified people."	More qualified than he is, at least.
"Far and away he looks like the best person for the job."	But up close…
"Our sales have been down in recent years. It's no surpriseQ he was promoted to sales manager." [44]	After he was promoted, sales took a nosedive.
"He's a man with driving ambitions."	He's partial to eighteen-wheelers.
"If I were you, I wouldn't hesitate to give him sweeping responsibilities."	He can also handle a mop.
"He's a steadyQ stable employee." [45]	He excels at cleaning the stalls and feeding the horses.
"Where could his talents be best used? I would say at the head of your departmental office."	…a born washroom attendant.

---

[44] For an explanation of the quomma (Q) and its uses, see p. 9.
[45] Ibid.

"She's excellent at taking orders."

She used to work at McDonald's, in fact.

"His enthusiasm is catching."

He always wanted to play for the Yankees.

"I see a brilliant career for him down the road."

...as a flagman at a highway construction site.

"When I last saw her, her business was just picking up."

...litter, mostly.

"He had no business training for this job."

He had no business doing *anything* relating to this job.

"He's a man of letters."

He's a mailman.

"I am pleased to recommend him for a new opportunity."

Overjoyed, in fact.

"He has an eye for pressing details."

He irons well.

"Since we hired him, we've never been happier."

...never happier than we were before we hired him, that is.

"He was in complete charge of both of our plants."

The ficus and the cactus.

"I'd have to describe his work as usually intense/in tents."[46]

He was a peanut vendor at the circus.

"He has an excellent track record."

No one's better at picking a winning horse.

"He's a goal-oriented type."

He's a wastepaper-basket hoopster.

---

[46] This phrase uses a homophone and works only for oral recommendations. For a discussion of homophones, see p. 95.

STUPIDITY

Recommendation	Meaning
"Nothing goes to his head."	If he were any denser, he'd have to be pruned.
"He spelled for me as department head on several occasions."	He had difficulty with words of more than five letters, though.
"Is he absorbed in his job? I can safely say that he is usually lost in his work."	...and with such a dazed look on his face.
"There is nothing you can teach a man like him."	He's utterly hopeless.
"She could never stay away from a project too long."	But we wish she would have stayed away longer.
"He has the mental faculties of a man twice his age."	He's bordering on premature senility.
"I would place his research on the cutting edge."	...of the shredder.
"She couldn't have done a better job for us."	Too bad, but she wasn't very bright.
"It seems that his potential clients always wind up giving him the business."	They always give him a hard time.

"You will find him among the most intelligent people you will ever meet."

He hangs around with bright people, but it just doesn't seem to rub off.

"He doesn't know the meaning of the word 'quit.'"

He can't spell it, either.

"He is not the type to just go by/buy the book." [47]

In fact, he can't even *read* the book.

"He's one of the few people here with half a brain."

We wonder what happened to the other half.

"His suggestions should not be tossed aside lightly." [48]

They should rather be thrown aside with great force.

"Hire him and you'll always have the complete dope on any subject."

Most ignorant person you'll ever meet.

"You will very much like himQ to say the least." [49]

Because every time he opens his mouth something silly comes out.

"His time here has been limited."

So also will his future.

---

[47] This phrase uses a homophone and works only for oral recommendations. For a discussion of homophones, see p. 95.

[48] This phrase is attributed to Dorothy Parker.

[49] For an explanation of the quomma (Q) and its uses, see p. 9.

"He has an awful lot of talent."	God-awful, actually.
"He worked like a fool for us."	How else would a fool work?
"He's the last person you'll want to consult when it comes to an important decision."	Don't even bother.
"He makes those he works with look even better."	Compared to him, *anyone* would look better.

UNEMPLOYABILITY

Recommendation	Meaning
"I can assure you that no one would be better for this job."	She is so unproductive that the position would be better left unfilled.
"After he left our firm last year, his job was to go begging for some time."	He spent his days panhandling.
"I am confident that no matter what task he undertakes, he will soon be fired with enthusiasm."	You'll eagerly have him cleaning out his desk before very long.
"Hire him and you'll not only get a serious man but a most educated one to boot."	...right out the door.
"We had nothing but concern for this woman."	...so we didn't hire her.
"When they made him, they threw away the mold."	It wasn't worth keeping.
"There were never too many complaints about his work."	There were lots of them and they were all justifiable.
"No salary would be too much for her."	Don't waste your money on her.

"I really cannot recall himQ never having done a good job for us."[50]

I'll never rehire him.

"She deserves no small part of the credit for the success of her division."

...not one iota, in fact.

"He's nobody's fool."

But if you hire him, he'll be your fool.

"He was a notable employee in the following ways: in/competent dealings with customers, in/articulate sales presentations, and in/considerate behavior toward his fellow employees."[51]

The guy's a zero any way you look at him.

"There's no mistaking this man's potential."

He has none.

"He was always at our disposal."

...which is exactly where you'll want to put him.

---

[50] For an explanation of the quomma (Q) and its uses, see p. 9.
[51] For an explanation of the space oddity (/), see p. 13.

"He'll go much faster than you expect."

He's never lasted anywhere very long.

"Is she good? Let me say that 'good' is not the word."

..."worthless" is, though.

"Our company wouldn't be what it is today had it not been for him."

It hurts to think about how much better off we'd be.

"We just couldn't wait to see what he could do."

Actually, we couldn't wait any longer—so we fired him.

"He is definitely *not* a has-been."

In fact, he's a "never was."

"The man's wisdom and sense of humor are qualities that we sorely missed."

He never had an ounce of either one.

"He's a man of few words."

...and even fewer smarts.

"He never quit anything that he started."

He was always fired first.

UNRELIABILITY

Recommendation	Meaning
"He had difficulty with his first assignment; but after that every other assignment turned out okay."	And the other half were disasters.
"He will work well under reasonable expectations."	Well under what anyone might reasonably expect.
"He usually goes after the most difficult task."	He can't get away quickly enough.
"He works like the devil."	He is the "Employee from Hell."
"There was no end to the tasks he would undertake for us."	He never finished his assignments.
"She will readily clutch at every major opportunity."	She gets so nervous she falls apart.
"He would take on every task with complete abandon."	He always gave up.
"Almost nothing could keep her from her work."	She's easily distracted.
"The most insignificant detail never escaped his attention."	He labored over petty matters.

"He's a promising worker."

...promising to get it right next time, promising not to be late again, promising to stay awake at his desk...

"It was a wonder how he ever managedQ putting as much time as he did into his outside interests." [52]

How could he supervise anyone? He was almost never at the office.

"She'll nod whenever you ask her to do something."

She has such a hard time keeping her eyes open at work.

"We never thought it was possible for reports to read like his did."

It was Bizarre-o-world.

"He really did know/no good work when he saw it." [53]

None at all.

"Her oversight was critical."

It cost us $2 million.

"Each report he wrote for us was better than the next."

They got worse each time.

---

[52] For an explanation of the quomma (Q) and its uses, see p. 9.
[53] This phrase uses a homophone and works only for oral recommendations. For a discussion of homophones, see p. 95.

MISCELLANY

Recommendation	Meaning
"Words cannot sufficiently express the amount of respect I have for his abilities."	But maybe "none at all" is close enough.
"It is not very difficult to argue against the contention that without him we would hardly have been in the position we are in today."	I have absolutely no idea what this statement is saying.
"I am confident that he will make a lasting impression wherever he decides to settle."	The impression his three-hundred-pound bulk left on our sofa lasted for weeks.
"He's a striking individual."	He's not shy about putting in time on the picket line.
"The fact that he got his foot in that client's door was amazing. I would have to call his feat/feet prodigious." [54]	Size 16E, at least.
"Relative to many other managers in our firm, this man has a great future in store for him."	He's related to the president, the vice-president, the treasurer, etc.

---

[54] This phrase uses a homophone and works only for oral recommendations. For a discussion of homophones, see p. 95.

"You won't often see her refuse."

She is very careful about hiding her trash.

"She would usually light up whenever we gave her more responsibility."

She must have smoked three packs a day.

"Is he a good credit risk? Let me just say that the attention he gives to his bills is unremitting."

He owes every creditor in town.

"He's the kind of person you will lean on when you have a problem."

He usually succumbs to pressure.

"His reaction to fellow workers in need of assistance is moving."

He'll just walk away.

"She always has the time for her fellow workers."

She loves to show off her Rolex.

"She's a far-sighted member of our management team."

She can't see a thing without her glasses.

"At any rate, you'll find he will work hard at his job."

You can pay him anything and he'll take it.

"She has no obvious weaknesses."

But a closer inspection will reveal quite a few.

"He came after me at our firm, so I didn't get to know him well." | I had to run for my life.

"He will be a definite addition to your staff." | Well, uh, okay.

"She had a/cute vision when it came to our financial planning." [55] | She thought we should have a bake sale.

"He has a rugged appearance." | He wears a hairpiece.

"She has everything going for her." | Her friends are going, her mind is going, her...

"He was in sales for several years before being kicked upstairs." | Actually, we felt like kicking him all over the place.

"I can't think of a better person for the job." | There are probably a million people better qualified, but right now I simply can't think of any.

---

[55] For an explanation of the space oddity (/), see p. 13.

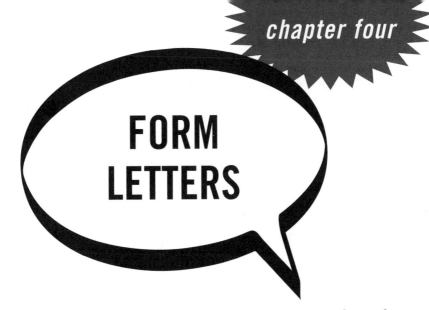

chapter four

FORM LETTERS

You might consider it thoughtless to use a ready-made ambiguous form letter for a recommendation. But almost anyone who's ever written more than one letter of recommendation probably has borrowed words, phrases, and whole sentences from previously written letters. And why not? After spending hours on a great opening sentence, on a "just right" set of compliments, and on a punchy closing line, why reinvent the wheel with every new letter you write? Besides, many people nowadays occasionally use ambiguous stock phrases to describe persons, places, and things. For example, how many eulogies have you sniffled through and heard, "All our lives are a little bit richer for having known the departed"? (Funny, but I usually can't recall being mentioned in the will.)

This chapter contains a sampling of form letters, each including many phrases and sentences from the lexicon in the previous chapter. Each one is preceded by a short description of the work habits, character, and traits of a hypothetical person. To use the letters, simply select the one that corresponds most closely to the person you're recommending. Okay, so the match isn't perfect. Add a few more ambiguous phrases of your own. (Be sure to mind your quommas.) Or how about adding some honest-to-goodness straight praise?! What's the problem with you, anyway? Can't you say *anything* nice about a person?

FORM LETTER A
For a Lazy and Unambitious Fellow Employee

Mal Inger just called and asked you for a letter of recommendation. Taken completely by surprise, you consented. Inger used to work with you several years ago. You didn't care for him very much. He was lazy and unambitious, and left you with the lion's share of the work whenever you struggled together on a project. Afterward, however, he would take most of the credit. In fact, at one time you were so angry with him you fantasized (while watching an old Al Capone movie) about putting out a contract on him. But why not put out a letter of recommendation like this one instead? It's much less expensive than a contract (except, perhaps, in Chicago).

Dear _____:

I understand that Mr. Mal Inger is interested in the possibility of employment with your firm. Mal has asked me to write a letter of recommendation, and I have cheerfully consented.

I am pleased to say that Mal is a former colleague of mine. We were employed with the same firm several years ago and worked together on several projects during that time. Once he put his mind to his work; nothing could stop him. He would never think twice about attacking a difficult problem, and he always seemed to find a way out of it.

Mal has confided to me that he is workingQ for a changeQ in his job. I honestly feel that you will be very lucky to get him to work for you. And Mal? I think he would like nothing better.

Sincerely yours,

_____

FORM LETTER B
For a Very Disagreeable Person

Ms. Marian Haste worked as your executive secretary last year. What a sourpuss! She was always in a foul mood, never smiled, and rarely had a nice word to say to anyone. Once, when you brought her flowers during National Secretary Week, she simply scowled and said, "So who died?" Since that time, you only remember her during National Pickle Week.

Some say she wasn't always as miserable as when you knew her. Rumor has it that she was once engaged to a man that she had known for only a few weeks. Shortly afterward he disappeared, leaving her a note explaining that he was suddenly called off on a five-year mission to explore strange new worlds. (He apparently signed up for several extra tours of duty.) Others say Marian is a Chicago Cubs fan. Unfortunately, if the latter rumor bears any truth, there is little hope for her recovery.

Marian has recently written to you and asked for a recommendation for a new job. What do you say?

Dear _____:

I understand that Ms. Marian Haste is under consideration for a job with your firm. I am pleased to say that I used to work with Ms. Haste, and I have consented to write this letter of recommendation for her.

I don't think you will find many people like Ms. Haste. Whatever work we gave her, she was always trying. Her advice, moreover, was always freely given and absolutely critical.

Most of the people who worked with Marian thought she took a lot of enjoyment out of work. Her coworkers had so much affection for her that almost everybody called her Mother. How much has she been missed since she left? Well, recently I heard several of her former colleagues say that they would love to see a portrait of her hanging in the office where she used to work.

When Marian left our firm, it was a crying shame. It's sad to see people like her leaving. However, I sincerely hope that she will go a long way in her new career.

Sincerely,

_____

FORM LETTER C
For a Dishonest Student

Fast Eddy Duperey was probably the most dishonest student you ever encountered. Although he had the brains to succeed in school, he partied and boogied away his four years at Watsamatta U. The word from other students is that he cheated on every exam he ever took. Sometimes he would write formulas on the soles of his shoes (he was double-jointed). Other times he would transcribe his notes on toilet-paper rolls in the washroom before a test (this is *not* easy to do); then, during the exam, he would feign an intestinal disorder and ask to be excused. After talking about Fast Eddy with other professors, you surmised that over four years he must have attended forty funerals for his grandparents, who died suddenly during final-exam weeks.

Fast Eddy's academic achievements could be written on the back of a postage stamp, but now he wants to go to law school. And he's asked you, "the professor who inspired him most," to write a letter of recommendation.

You should have said, "No way," you coward, but you developed a sudden case of marshmallowitis. This letter ought to bail you out.

Dear _____:

Mr. Edward Duperey has applied for admission to your College of Law. He has asked me, as one of his professors, to write a letter of recommendation for him.

I have known Mr. Duperey for three years, having first encountered him as a student in my statistics class. His grade in the course was only average; however, I would have to say his true ability is deceiving. He is definitely a young man to watch. Most of the other professors who know Ed agree that one day he will forge a name for himself.

Mr. Duperey always found his course work challenging. In fact, once he put his mind to his work, nothing could stop him. He couldn't care less about the hours of study his courses required of him.

All in all, I cannot recommend Mr. Duperey highly enough. I would venture to say that he will do well in any law school with no qualifications whatsoever.

Sincerely yours,

_____

FORM LETTER D
For a Bad Dude

Des Perado worked for your company last year. He hasn't a decent bone in his entire body. He always seems to be in trouble, and was arrested a number of times while he worked for you. In fact, he was once allegedly observed breaking into your safe after hours, but the night watchman later came down with a sudden case of amnesia.

Mr. Perado has an arrest record a mile long—not just for the usual burglary, robbery, and arson, but also for pillaging, sacking, and plundering. (You *know* this guy is bad; the last ones to commit crimes like this were the Visigoths.) Why weren't you aware of his background before you hired him? Funny how all of his letters of recommendation were very positive.

Des took an unpaid leave of absence from your firm last year. He said he'd be gone for six months (maybe less with "good behavior"). Now he has requested a letter of recommendation for a new job. Somehow you find it hard to refuse him.

Dear _____:

Mr. Des Perado has informed me that he is being considered for a position with your firm. As his former employer, I have been asked to write a letter of recommendation for him.

Mr. Perado worked for us several years ago. While he was in our employ, he was given several citations. As far as his integrity is concerned, I will simply point out that he has a long and notable record.

You will probably see that he has held quite a few jobs over the past few years and that his work record is intermittent. I am sure Mr. Perado will be the first one to tell you that many of the other places where he spent his time were too confining, and that he wanted to break out of them.

If I were you, I would not think twice about giving him a position entailing financial responsibility. In fact, during his time with us he had a hand in our company's financial dealings. For the job that he did, we now find ourselves deeply indebted. I'm sorry we let him get away.

Sincerely,

_____

FORM LETTER E
For an Employee with a Poor Attendance Record

Billy Bob Bumphus was employed with your firm for a month last year. Never in your many years of experience have you seen a man so ill-suited to work. His absentee record was...well, a record for your firm. When he did show up, he bungled every task assigned to him. Finally, he stopped coming to work altogether. Just last week you saw him again, panhandling down by the bus terminal. Incredibly, Billy Bob said he's got a chance at a new job and asked you for a letter of recommendation. How about this one?

Dear _____:

Mr. William Robert Bumphus has asked me to write a letter of recommendation for him. I have been informed that he is under consideration for employment with your company.

Mr. Bumphus worked for us for a short time last year, but unfortunately I cannot remember the exact dates. Quite frankly, he is not your normal everyday employee, and a man like him is hard to find. In fact, after he left us, his job was to go begging for nearly a year.

When Mr. Bumphus was with our firm, there really wasn't very much workQ which he couldn't do. I think now that his principal interest all along was lying in the supply room. In any case, I suggest that you not hesitate to give him sweeping responsibilities. We did, and it worked out quite well.

If you would like to hear more about Mr. Bumphus, please call. All in all, I urge you to waste no time in making him an offer of employment.

Sincerely,

_____

FORM LETTER F
For the Office Drunk

John Philip Souse will imbibe anything—beer, wine, liquor, and even (it is rumored) the bottle of mouthwash he keeps in his desk drawer. Like most problem drinkers, he denies that he is an alcoholic, but why then does that bottle of mouthwash have an olive in it?

Recently you've instituted a smoking ban among your office personnel. Your action was hailed as a bold step for the rights of nonsmokers; but you have told no one the real reason: fear of an explosion and flash fire if John Philip should happen to sneeze while someone was lighting up.

His heavy drinking has taken its toll on his work performance, and you have had several run-ins with him over it. Now he has been giving some thought to changing employers. Here is your chance to say everything you've ever wanted to say about him...sort of...in a letter.

Dear _____:

Mr. John Philip Souse is, I understand, under serious consideration for a position with your firm. He has asked me, as his supervisor, to write a letter of recommendation concerning his work experience here.

John has been employed with us for the last ten years. He has a flair for writing clear, concise reports. The number of reports he can produce in a day, while staggering, does not accurately reflect his ability, since he often finds it necessary to go through several drafts before he thinks a report sounds just right. In any case, he always seems to be loaded with work to do.

I'm not sure why John is thinking of resigning his current position. In all honesty, though, I think his real talent may be getting wasted here. If he does leave, however, I will always think of the times he spent working for us as happy hours. The impression other people have of him is invariably high.

If I can provide any further information, please do not hesitate to call.

Sincerely,

_____

FORM LETTER G
For a Perfectly Average, Dull Fellow

Norm Humdrum is giving you fits. He's asked you for a letter of recommendation, but everything about him is so *ordinary*. He had a straight C average in college, does fair-to-middling work for your company, and gets an average raise every year. His personal life? He has an average-size family (1.9 children), wears a bow tie, drives a Corolla, and lives in a suburb of Cleveland.

How do you write an honest recommendation that would get anyone excited about hiring this guy?

Dear _____:

Mr. Norman Humdrum is interested in being considered for employment with your firm. As Mr. Humdrum's friend and coworker for the last several years, I am happy to write this letter.

When Norm walks into his office in the morning, he comes to work. In fact, he'll never fail to give you a fair day's work. He deserves—and has received—just recognition as part of our work team.

Norm is also a man of vision when it comes to seeing what has to be done. Most of his coworkers would agree with me when I say that he has a real head on his shoulders. He also has an eye for detail, and he worksQ wellQ with others.

All in all, I can say nothingQ contrary to what his résumé shows. I strongly suggest that he be considered eligible for the position he is seeking. I am confident that the time and money you invest in Mr. Humdrum will beQ wellQ spent.

Sincerely,

_____

FORM LETTER H
For the Office Playboy

Lance Studd boasts that he knows every woman in the firm. (We're talking in the biblical sense here.) He likes to say that he believes in a "horizontal style of management," and laughs about how he "relates well" with his female coworkers. He also finds a hidden sexual meaning in everything. You find him disgusting.

Lance is being considered for a new position, and he's asked you for a recommendation. Why not let this letter do your talking?

Dear _____:

I understand that Mr. Lance Studd is under consideration for employment with your firm. I am pleased to be able to recommend him for this new opportunity.

What kind of person is he? I can safely say that he has always had pleasant relations with those under him. You'll also find that his reputation is in/decent dealings with all of his associates. He's a quiet type, and has been often laidQ back since the time when I first met him.

It was pleasant working with Lance for the short time that we did. He touched most everyone at our firm in so many ways. And I have the utmost confidence that he will make out on his new job.

Sincerely,

_____

FORM LETTER I
For an Absolute Good-for-Nothing

How about a letter for someone who has no redeeming work qualities at all? He is lazy, disagreeable, shiftless, a screw-up, and...he's got ring-around-the-collar. Here's a letter that will render justice to all those traits—for a Noah Count, a man your firm fired (with gusto) several months ago.

Dear _____:

I have been told that Mr. Noah Count is being considered for employment with your firm, and I am pleased to write this letter of recommendation for him.

Mr. Count was employed with our firm in the accounts division last year. A seasoned employee like Mr. Count is hard to find, and we had a difficult time replacing him. You won't find many people like Mr. Count. His fellow workers were always raving about his work. I honestly think that he could not have done a better job for us if he had tried.

Noah thinks little of hard work, and he didn't think much of the many extra hours he had to put in during our busy season, either. It seems that we could never give him too much to do.

Noah has informed me that he is ready to strike out in a new career and would like to work for you in the worst way. If you seriously consider his application, I am confident that you will find no one better for the position. And if you do hire him, I am certain that he will be fired with enthusiasm.

Sincerely,

_____

chapter five

TELEPHONE RECOMMENDATIONS

So now you have a stack of form letters to use for those difficult people you've had to work with over the years. That's the good news. The bad news is many people today prefer to give (and ask for) recommendations over the telephone. It's not surprising. You can give more information about someone in a shorter period of time over the phone. Also, with the rising tide of lawsuits, fewer people are willing to offer negative comments about someone if the comments won't remain confidential. The beauty of the phone recommendation is that it leaves no trace—unless, of course, your phone is bugged.

Oral communications have still another advantage over written ones—you can use vocal tricks. For example, a pause before an affirmative reply to the question, "Was he a reliable employee?" will leave the caller wondering what you really meant. Certain types of accent, inflection, and emphasis likewise can be befuddling. For example, compare the implication of the unaccented response to the previous question:

"I never had any problems with him." [A solid recommendation]

with that of the accented response:

"*I* never had any problems with him." [But others did.]

In this chapter, I provide a series of hints, tips, and suggestions for preparing yourself to give ambiguous telephone recommendations. I use examples from the lexicon in chapter 3, including homophones (homo-whats?). I will then discuss a handful (or should I say a mouthful?) of voice tricks that can be used effectively in telephone recommendations, such as pauses, gaps, and inflections. Finally, I will provide you with a set of suitably ambiguous responses to questions typically asked in telephone requests for employment recommendations.

Dodging the Call
R-r-r-ring

"Hello, this is Fred Smith with the Harpy Corporation. I'm calling in reference to Hugo Smedley, who I understand used to work for you. Mr. Smedley has put in an application for a job with us, and I'm wondering if you can spare a few moments to answer some questions about him. Your boss put me through directly to you."

What do you do first? Stall. Ask if you can call back. Never give a recommendation cold—even if it's a favorable one. Pausing to collect your thoughts and plan your remarks is especially important for an ambiguous recommendation.

Ideally, your first line of defense would be to have someone head off the call before it reaches you with the universal "I'm sorry, he's at a meeting right now." (I've always marveled at how anything gets done nowadays in the business world since it seems everyone is at a meeting virtually every moment of the day.)

If a call does get through, you'll have to give some reason for not talking. In my experience, the more befuddling the excuse, the more effectively it puts off the caller. One of my favorites goes like this: "Look, can I call you back? I'm in the middle of inverting a matrix." This usually confuses the caller, who is often too embarrassed to admit ignorance.

Esoteric excuses are still no *absolute* guarantee against a persistent caller insisting that he or she will only take a minute to ask some questions about Smedley. To guard against this possibility, you might try imitating a voice-mail message on an answering machine:

"Hello, this is _____. I'm not in the office right now but your call is important to me. [1] If you leave your name and number at the tone, I will get back to you as soon as I can."

Then in your finest falsetto—or castrato, if you're so (un)equipped—let fly with the signal.

---

[1] How can a call be important to you if you're not there to know who's calling? (Just a thought.)

Preparing Yourself

All right. Your diversion has worked and your party is going to call you back later. Now you have time to compose yourself—and your responses. What next? Well, just who was Hugo Smedley? Does he deserve a good recommendation, or one from the lexicon? If the latter, decide what you want to say and turn immediately to chapter 3. Remember that most of the ambiguous phrases and sentences that work well in a letter will also work quite nicely in an oral recommendation. The problem, though, is that you can't always control the drift of a phone conversation. You must be prepared to answer questions with an *immediate* ambiguous response.

Here's a technique that will work wonders: flashing. No, it's not what you think. I'm talking about flash*cards*. Remember the ones you used to memorize your multiplication tables? Well, regular practice with a set of flashcards will also help you develop a quick response. *L.I.A.R.* flashcards are easy to make. All you have to do is put together a list of questions most commonly asked of people giving employment recommendations. (Those from the telephone conversation on pp. 97–100 will do.) Then for each question, select one or two of your favorite sentences or phrases from chapter 3. Get a set of three-by-five-inch index cards. On each one, put a question on one side and a response on the other, such as:

<table>
<tr>
<td>"Does he need
a lot of
supervision?"</td>
<td>"Well, let me just say
that generally he
works without any
direction."</td>
</tr>
</table>

Telephone Tricks

You've stalled, you've studied, and so you're almost ready for the telephone interview. Now comes the interesting part. You actually have some new techniques to use—ones that aren't in the lexicon because they can't be used in written letters of recommendation. They're oral techniques— devices that I have dubbed "vocal vague-aries."

The Pause

First of all we have the pause, which might be called "the pause that perplexes." Take this example:

Q: "Would you say Smedley was an honest employee?"
A: ...[one thousand one, one thousand two]..."Yes."
Q: "You *would* say he was honest then?"
A: ...[one thousand three, one thousand four]..."Yes."

Caution: use the pause sparingly. If you don't, you'll come across sounding like you're not playing with a full deck.

The Word Drag

The word drag is a clever device that instills a bit of doubt in the mind of the listener as to whether the speaker really means what he says. Using the above example again:

Q: "Would you say Smedley was an honest employee?"
A: " ...mmmmmmmmmmyyyyyeeeessss."

If you can't read the above expression—which looks like a gaggle of letters on a roller-coaster ride—the dragged "yes" begins with a short, high-pitched "m" sound, followed by a drawn-out "yes" rising on a five-note crescendo. [2] Okay—now go back and practice (but close the doors and windows so nobody hears you). Word-dragging can be used most effectively with questions requiring a yes-or-no answer.

The Voice Gap

Voice gapping is yet another vocal technique that can be used effectively in oral recommendations. The voice gap is nothing but a very short pause in speaking and is the oral equivalent of the quomma, the schizocolon, or the space oddity. For example:

Here the voice gap stands for a space oddity:

Q: "In what way would you say that Smedley made the biggest impact on your firm?"

A: "I would say in (voice gap) competent handling of payroll accounts." .

Here the two voice gaps play the role of two quommas:

Q: "Would you comment on how he gets along with the rest of his colleagues?"

A: "Smedley works (voice gap) well (voice gap) with others."

The Accented Response

Another vocal vague-ary—the accented response—has already been mentioned at the beginning of this chapter.

---

[2] If this is too confusing, the voice modulation described above for the affirmative word drag is almost identical to that used by the Big Bopper in his "H-e-l-l-o-o-o Baby."

Suppose the question was asked: "How would you rate his learning ability?"

Compare the meaning implied by the unaccented response: "I would say that he has remarkable learning ability." (a very positive recommendation.) with the meaning implied by the accented response:

"I would say that he has remarkable learning *ability*" (but whether he uses his ability is another matter altogether).

The Bad Connection

When you use vocal vague-aries, you run the risk of having to clarify your answer. "Just what do you mean by that?" the caller might ask. (This is a decided disadvantage of the telephone recommendation.) If you're desperate, you might try the most drastic telephone trick of all: the bad connection. Depressing the disconnect button lightly several times can give the illusion of a temporary disconnection. Continuing to speak while you are depressing the button helps to heighten the effect.

You can use this trick to destroy the questioner's train of thought if he or she has asked you to clarify a response. You can also selectively delete certain syllables—or even whole words—to make a bad recommendation sound good. I'll let your imagination run here.

Homophones

Another great device for oral recommendations is the homophone. Most people are more familiar with the term "homonyms"—words that sound alike but are spelled differently—and kids love to see how many they can think up:

"road" and "rode," for example, "right" and "write," and many more. The more precise term for such words, however, is "homophone," meaning same-sounding.

How can homophones be used in intentionally ambiguous recommendations? Easily, as the following examples show. When asked how much respect an employee's coworkers have for him, you might say:

> "The breadth of the man is overwhelming and quite obvious to anyone working closely with him."

That's quite a compliment...unless you use a homophone for "breadth," which would then turn the comment into:

> "The breath of the man is overwhelming and quite obvious to anyone working closely with him."

What's your meaning? He's got the worst halitosis you've ever run up against.

Or how about the following:

> "He was sometimes cited at his former job."

This implies that the worker probably received recognition as Employee of the Month; Top Salesman, Eastern Region; or something like that. Right? But substitute a homophone for "cited" and you get:

> "He was sometimes sighted at his former job."

With the homophone substitute, the statement implies

that this character probably stayed home more often than he showed up for work.

Or to use one more example, in answer to the question:

"How would you describe his salary level?"

you might respond:

"I'll just say I wouldn't have minded having his salary."

Sounds like we're talking about a highly paid executive? But substitute a homophone and we get:
"I'll just say I wouldn't have minded halving his salary."

Homophonically speaking, this guy was paid twice as much as he was worth.

As you might have noted already, the lexicon in chapter 3 contains a generous helping of homophones. For the definitive source, however, consult James B. Hobbs's *Homophones and Homographs: An American Dictionary.* [3]

A Telephone Conversation

Let's wrap up our discussion of these devices with an example of a telephone conversation. Many personnel management consultants suggest that a standard series of questions be asked about a job applicant. The following hypothetical telephone conversation is based on fifteen commonly asked questions. In response to the questions, I

---

[3] James B. Hobbs, *Homophones and Homographs: An American Dictionary*, 3rd edition, Jefferson, N.C. and London: MacFarlane, 1999.

have selected a number of appropriate responses from the lexicon in chapter 3. The double meanings—when unclear—are in brackets. I've also liberally interspersed vocal vague-aries. Here goes:

Caller: "Good morning, this is Fred Smith of the Harpy Corporation again. I hope you've finished subverting your matron. Do you have time to talk about Hugo Smedley now?"

You: "Sure, Fred. As we say in human resources, 'Fire away.'"

Caller: "What were his responsibilities when he worked for you?"

You: "There weren't many tasks (voice gap) which he couldn't do, so we gave him sweeping responsibilities."

Caller: "What kind of supervision did he require?"

You: "He generally worked without any direction at all."

Caller: "Did he work well as part of a team?"

You: "No matter what project he was involved in, his coworkers told me that his input was always critical. Also, they felt that he deserved no small part of the credit for his team's overall success."

Caller: "Did any work conflicts that involved him ever arise?"

You: "Most of the employees I spoke to said that they were happy working with him for the short time that they did. I was also told that I wouldn't find too many other workers like him."

Caller: "What about his attendance record? Was it a good one?"

You: "'*Good*' is hardly the word. A man like Smedley is extremely hard to find."

Caller: "Can you discuss some of Mr. Smedley's major strengths?"

You: "I can mention several ways in which he stood out among other workers: in (voice gap) accurate reports, in (voice gap) capable handling of accounts, and in (voice gap) considerate behavior toward his fellow staffers."

Caller: "Does Mr. Smedley have any significant weaknesses?"

You: "I really can't say anything critical about him. [I'm afraid of getting sued.] But I will say that I think his real talent was getting wasted at work."

Caller: "How would you describe his learning ability?"

You: "His capacity for learning is actually nothing (voice gap) which should be laughed at. We soon learned that no job was too much for this man to handle."

Caller: "How would you compare his record with those of others with similar duties and responsibilities?"

You: "Let me assure you that no one would have been better for the job."

Caller: "Could I ask you the reasons he left your firm?"

You: "He was ready to strike out in a new career. The last time we spoke about it I saw that he was fired with enthusiasm."

Caller: "Did you replace him after he left?"

You: "After he left, his job was to go begging. I'm inclined to believe now that no one will ever replace him."

Caller: "Could you tell me what salary your firm paid him?"

You: "Without getting too much into specifics, just let me say that I wouldn't have minded halving his salary."

Caller: "Given your experience with the applicant and knowing his qualifications, would you hire him again?"

You: "I wouldn't think twice about hiring this man again. He has my unqualified endorsement."

Caller: "Thank you very much for your time. You've given me a lot of solid information about Mr. Smedley. It sounds like you lost a valuable employee when he left."

You: "You'll be lucky to get him to work for you."

chapter six

THE OTHER FOOT

So far, all of our attention has been on the provider of a recommendation. I've shown you verbal sleight-of-hand, introduced you to hundreds of ambiguous phrases, written form letters just right for that "special someone," and even supplied you with ways to give tele-phoney recommendations. "Great fun! Witty! Ha-Ha," you might be thinking. But wait! What if it's you who's the subject of the letter? What if you're the one who's being given an "unqualified" recommendation? Or the one whose true ability is "deceiving?" Not so funny anymore, is it?

Look, everyone makes mistakes. So yours lasted a little longer than most. Maybe you partied your way through college. Or you've fallen asleep at work so often that your boss has suggested having an airbag installed at your desk. Perhaps you've been axed from so many jobs that you dream you're running from a guy named Jason in a goalie mask. But now you've seen the light. You're sick of cleaning out your desk, and you're determined to clean up your act. The problem is, how can you put your miserable record behind you—or, if that's impossible, how can you make it seem not so bad?

Despair not. In this chapter we turn the tables. I will fill you in on ways to shine up that less-than-stellar record and make you—a bozo (no offense?)—come across looking like an Iacocca!

Should You Lie?

Absolutely not. In fact, if you've been paying close attention so far, you've surely noticed that the whole point of the book has been how to give an honest recommendation. It's just been the case that the recommendations in this book can all be interpreted as either good ones or bad ones. Despite the acronym title of this book, you should never be dishonest about your background or work experience. There are several reasons why. First, lies are…well, they're naughty. And second, employers are catching on! Résumé lying is clearly on the rise, but employers are increasingly checking up on résumés or claims that look suspicious or implausible.[1] And it doesn't take much digging to check whether a degree was really earned or whether that grade point average was really a 4.0. Furthermore, although most lies are told early in a career to "get a foot in the door," they leave a trail that is hard to erase as people move up the ladder.

So Then?…

So what do you do? The first thing to realize is that many of the ambiguous phrases in the lexicon in chapter 3 can work

---

[1] Del Jones, "Résumé Boosting Can Bust Careers," *USA Today*, September 13, 1996, p. 2B.

in two ways. Providers of recommendations can use them, *or*—with just a little reworking—they can be used by...oops ...I was going to refer to you by that B-word again, but hold on.

Let's get a new term that doesn't immediately call to mind images of circus music or quarter pounders with cheese. How about one whose record is "well under maximum potential"—which acronymizes to WUMP. It's much nicer being called a Wump rather than a bozo, isn't it? Good. Now let's continue.

As an example, suppose that you feel it would be impressive to mention something on your résumé about the wide-ranging responsibilities that you could handle, even though at your last job you only pushed a broom. You could always put in the "Previous Experience" section of your résumé:

"At my former position, I was entrusted with sweeping responsibilities."

Or remember when your coworker went on vacation for three weeks and asked you to water that African violet on her desk? Isn't it then perfectly truthful to put on your résumé:

"I was placed in sole charge of the plant for three weeks last year."

See how easy it is?

Unfortunately, there are some wumpisms that not even the lexicon phrases can make look good. Furthermore, some prospective employers might be wily enough to see right through the double meanings that the phrases convey. After all, since this book will no doubt sell one billion copies, it is only a matter of time until the various lexicon entries become so well known to employers that they lose their effectiveness. What do you do then?

Fortunately, there's another device—a secret weapon—that I haven't told you about yet. That device? Politically correct (or P.C.) phraseology. Everyone's familiar with the movement for politically correct speech. It is considered insensitive, for example, to refer to a person who is only four and one half feet tall as "short." Instead, that person is said to be "vertically challenged." And it's not nice to describe a person's appearance as "homely" or "ugly" but rather as "differently attractive." I've even heard that the term preferred by some for a dead person is "necro-American." Although the movement for politically correct speech has certainly drawn a lot of debate, that is not our concern here. The point is simply that you can formulate "P.C." descriptions to make your own wumpish failings seem less negative, less detracting, and less unflattering on your résumé or in your job-application letter. Here are a few examples:

- If your employer quizzes you about your poor attendance record at your last job, you don't have to apologetically say, "Yeah, I guess I missed a lot of days." Instead, you could simply say that you did in fact "maintain a regular dispresence at work." Sounds much better, doesn't it?
- Or if you had the misfortune of spending a couple of days in jail for amassing fifty thousand parking tickets, don't just admit that you did time in the city slammer.

Instead, put it this way: "I've expanded my horizons through experiencing an alternative restricted lifestyle."

- Or suppose that you were fired from your last job. Instead of confessing that you were let go, simply say that you were "permanently leisured."

I'm not going to furnish you with a complete set of P.C. descriptions for various wumpy characteristics—that could take up a whole new lexicon. However, I have provided you with a short list on the next couple of pages to get you started. You'll soon find that it's very easy to make up your own.

Some Politically Correct Descriptions for Selected Wumpisms

Wumpism	*P.C. Description*
"I had a poor attendance record at my last job."	"I maintained a regular dispresence at work."
"I missed a lot of days of work."	"I was ofttimes workplace-removed."
"I was frequently late."	"I respect alternative principles of punctuality."
"I've got a drinking problem."	"I have conducted considerable research of an experiential nature on the brewing industry."

"I've been arrested a few times."

"I have interfaced with luminaries of the law-enforcement community."

"I've spent time in jail."

"I have expanded my horizons through experiencing an alternative restricted lifestyle."

"I've been caught lying."

"I have been acknowledged as truth-challenged."

"I was accused of padding my expenses."

"I have a predisposition to creativity and originality in the numerical domain."

"I've been caught stealing."

"I have been formally recognized in the area of disownership."

"I've been evaluated as 'lazy' on my performance appraisal."

"I possess an immunity to motivational stimuli."

"I was downgraded."

"I was differently promoted."

"I was fired from my last job."

"I was permanently leisured."

"I've been out of work for two years."

"I have been continuously nonsalaried."

"I squeaked by with barely passing grades in school."

"My academic record is one of superior nonachievement."

The Big Interview

Sooner or later, you're going to have to face the music in a job interview. Whether that music is going to sound like a love song or a swan song (or maybe even a death march!) is up to you and the answers you give in that all-important interview.

In the remainder of this chapter, I've created the Job Interview from Hell—a nightmare interview with killer questions and appropriate lexicon and P.C. responses to these questions. Okay, I'm exaggerating—the questions aren't all that bad. It's your record, your performance at school, and your previous job experience that's the nightmare. But maybe the responses I've tendered can help bail you out.

Interviewer: "Welcome, Mr. Smedley. I look forward to an interesting interview. What name would you prefer that I call you by?"

Helpful Hint No. 1: It's not a good idea to let on that you have a nickname. Monikers like "Butch," "Ace," —or even worse, given-name/nickname combinations like "Willie the Weasel" or "Frankie Fingers"—generally aren't going to impress an interviewer (unless he has one, too). Also, if you have a rather unusual-sounding name like Billy Bob or Bubba Joe, either use only initials (like W. Robert or B. Joseph) or else just turn around and walk out the door.

You: "Hugo is fine."

Interviewer: "I see you're no longer with the Harpy Corporation?"

You: [Gulp. I just got canned.] "That's correct. I guess you could say that I was fired with considerable enthusiasm, and it consequently had, well, a moving effect on me."

Interviewer: "I see that you're a graduate of Lemming University. How well did you do there?"

You: [Yikes—I squeaked by with barely passing grades.] "I'm proud to say that my scholastic accomplishments reflect what I would call maximum potential nonperformance."

Helpful Hint No. 2: If you're a fresh college graduate, your résumé would usually also list your GPA (grade point average). But what if your GPA is so low that it looks like the line score of a shutout ballgame? One possibility is to convert your GPA to natural logarithms (and change the sign). On second thought, if your GPA is really that low, you probably don't know what a natural logarithm is. Forget this advice.

Interviewer: "What degree were you awarded?"

You: "My degree? It was, uh, B.S."

Helpful Hint No. 3: Some people today who have received several degrees (e.g., a bachelor's and a master's) like to list their degree initials after their names. If you are such a person, be sure to make sure that the "degree tail" after your name is not one that makes you look ridiculous. Here are some degree tails you should definitely avoid:

M.A.M.A.—(two master of arts degrees)

M.A.M.B.A.—(one M.A. and one M.B.A. Also, a poisonous snake)

B.A.M.A.—(With a degree tail like this, expect an interviewer to ask about your banjo.)

B.A.A.A.—(a very unfortunate bachelors/associate-of-arts degree combination)

B.A.L.L.D.—(I'd suggest putting the doctor-of-laws degree (LL.D.) before the B.A.)

D.O.L.L.B.A.B.—(My advice for those with a bachelor of arts (A.B.) and a bachelor of laws (LL.B.) degree is not to pursue that doctor of osteopathy (D.O.) degree—especially if your name is Barbie or Ken)

Interviewer: "Did you graduate with honors?"

You: "Well, it's not on my résumé, but I'm a *nulla cum laude* graduate." [2]

---

[2] *Nulla cum laude* is Latin for "with no distinction whatsoever." Before using this it might be a good idea to first determine if your interviewer knows any Latin. One way of doing this is to greet him or her with a hearty "salve!" (hail) rather than a "hello," and then watch carefully for a puzzled expression.

Interviewer: "Have you had any experience supervising people?"

You: "Well, at Harpy it just didn't happen that I was promoted to a management position after only six months on the job."

Interviewer: "I hear that your former firm has had a very profitable last few years. What kind of role do you think you played?"

You: "In all modesty, I played no small role in Harpy's success. And I doubt that there is anyone who would fail to deny my not inconsiderable contributions to the firm."

Interviewer: "How much responsibility were you given for major projects?"

You: "I think it's safe to say that my oversight was of the highest importance." [In fact, my oversight lost a major account.]

Interviewer: "How well would you say you express yourself? I'm referring to your communications skills, of course."

You: "Well, I have a flair for writing." [It's a red one.]

Interviewer: "What would you say your strongest suit is?"

You: [My strongest suit? It's the polyester one I bought at the thrift shop—my only suit.] "My former boss once told me about the way in which I stood out among his other employees: most notably, in/sane advice that I always gave him."

Interviewer: "How well do you deal with change?"

You: "I have absolutely no difficulty handling change." [When I worked at the amusement arcade, it was the big bills that gave me trouble.]

Interviewer: "We're a firm that puts a lot of importance in our employees being on time every day. How can you convince me that you can live up to our high standards of punctuality and attendance?"

You: "Well, my former boss had said that his worries were over when I began to work for him. And I'd also like to just state for the record that I'm a man who never misses work."

Interviewer: "I noticed on your résumé that your references would be available upon request. Could you provide me with their names and how I might contact them?"

You: "Of course. Here is a list. I'm sure you'll find that all of my references will give me their unqualified endorsement."

Helpful Hint No. 4: With your record, you might have difficulty rounding up a good set of references. If this is the case, you might consider listing your mom and dad—but first check with them to make sure that they will give you a good recommendation. Also, listing only deceased references (oops, I mean necro-Americans) is a sure way of preventing unfavorable recommendations.

Interviewer: "How well do you get along with your fellow workers? I'd appreciate a straight answer here."

You: [Gulp. My coworkers used to send me hate email— or is it e-hate-mail?] "Well, all I can say is that when I left my last job, my boss said that I was a difficult man to replace. He also said that he'd seen very few people like me."

Interviewer: "I hope you don't mind my bluntness. Have you ever had any problems involving alcohol that affected your work performance?"

You: "I don't drink any more." [I don't drink any less, either. But I think I'll have one after this interview.]

Interviewer: "Well, let's wrap things up. I like the way you handle yourself with these tough questions, Smedley. I think there's a good chance you'll be hearing from us."

You: "Thank you, sir. I'd like nothing better."

AFTERWORD

If you've read this far, you're well on the road to mastering the craft of providing ambiguous recommendations. What advantages will you enjoy? Well, first of all, you'll never again have fits of anxiety about giving a recommendation for someone who is best described as "beyond the pail." Also, once your prowess becomes known, you'll probably never be asked to write another recommendation. This alone is worth the price of the book. [1]

Furthermore, after reading this book you may well gain a sharper awareness of just how many ambiguities—so many of them delightful and absurd—rain down upon us in our daily lives. Unfortunately, sniffing out these ambiguities has become for me an obsession—or maybe even a disease. For example, I've noticed:

---

[1] To promote this great value, I respectfully suggest that you purchase several hundred copies of this book and distribute them to your friends and acquaintances.

- A wily politician who responds to a tough question by saying: "I can't agree with you more."
- A sign in the park that says: "Fine for littering."
- A student who is quoted in the campus newspaper as saying: "It always amazes me how many students can develop a good relationship with the faculty."
- A candidate for political office who says: "I'm running again because I don't think I've done enough good things."
- A student who is quoted as saying: "An M.B.A. degree will provide me with the type of education on which no value can be placed."
- A newspaper ad for a house that "won't last long."
- A former elected official who reasons: "It's difficult to believe that people in this country are starving because food isn't available."
- The business student who writes that his specialty is "MIS/Management."

And so it goes....

About the Author

Robert J. Thornton is a professor of economics at Lehigh University in Bethlehem, Pennsylvania. Over the years, he has lost much sleep worrying how to write fitting letters of recommendation. His colleagues at Lehigh have grown weary listening to him talk about the subject, however, and wish he would get a life. For obvious reasons, he seldom is asked to write letters of recommendation any more, and he is deathly afraid to ask anyone to write one for him.